797,885 Books
are available to read at

Forgotten Books

www.ForgottenBooks.com

Forgotten Books' App
Available for mobile, tablet & eReader

ISBN 978-0-260-69133-0
PIBN 11115981

This book is a reproduction of an important historical work. Forgotten Books uses state-of-the-art technology to digitally reconstruct the work, preserving the original format whilst repairing imperfections present in the aged copy. In rare cases, an imperfection in the original, such as a blemish or missing page, may be replicated in our edition. We do, however, repair the vast majority of imperfections successfully; any imperfections that remain are intentionally left to preserve the state of such historical works.

Forgotten Books is a registered trademark of FB &c Ltd.
Copyright © 2017 FB &c Ltd.
FB &c Ltd, Dalton House, 60 Windsor Avenue, London, SW19 2RR.
Company number 08720141. Registered in England and Wales.

For support please visit www.forgottenbooks.com

1 MONTH OF FREE READING

at
www.ForgottenBooks.com

By purchasing this book you are eligible for one month membership to ForgottenBooks.com, giving you unlimited access to our entire collection of over 700,000 titles via our web site and mobile apps.

To claim your free month visit:
www.forgottenbooks.com/free1115981

* Offer is valid for 45 days from date of purchase. Terms and conditions apply.

English
Français
Deutsche
Italiano
Español
Português

www.forgottenbooks.com

Mythology Photography **Fiction**
Fishing Christianity **Art** Cooking
Essays Buddhism Freemasonry
Medicine **Biology** Music **Ancient Egypt** Evolution Carpentry Physics
Dance Geology **Mathematics** Fitness
Shakespeare **Folklore** Yoga Marketing
Confidence Immortality Biographies
Poetry **Psychology** Witchcraft
Electronics Chemistry History **Law**
Accounting **Philosophy** Anthropology
Alchemy Drama Quantum Mechanics
Atheism Sexual Health **Ancient History**
Entrepreneurship Languages Sport
Paleontology Needlework Islam
Metaphysics Investment Archaeology
Parenting Statistics Criminology
Motivational

Historic, archived document

Do not assume content reflects current
scientific knowledge, policies, or practices.

EGYPTIAN COTTON NEWS LETTER
(Not for publication)

By Office of Egyptian Cotton Breeding, Bureau of Plant
Industry, U. S. Department of Agriculture.

The information contained in this News Letter is drawn mainly
from newspapers and trade journals, the published source of the
information being given in every case. The object of the letter
is to furnish information to officials and cooperators of the
Department of Agriculture in regard to the condition of the market
for long staple cotton. The Department assumes no responsibility
for the accuracy and reliability of these quoted statements, and
under no circumstances should they be republished as having been
issued by the Department of Agriculture.

LONG STAPLE COTTON MARKET CONDITIONS

The New Bedford Standard of February 1 states as follows:

"Extra staple cotton markets here and elsewhere in New England
became more active this week following several weeks in succession
of active trading in the gray goods markets. Purchases of raw
material usually came in small lots, but there was dealing in so
many different quarters of the market that the sales total for
the week reached very respectable proportions. Inquiry, moreover,
continued sufficiently active at the close of the week to give every
ground for expecting further continuation of the trading, since the
business so far booked is far from adequate to cover all the new
cloth and yarn orders taken during the past two or three weeks.
           *   *   *

"There has been comparatively little activity in the longer types,
and sales of cotton longer than inch and three-sixteenths have been
few and far between. ***
           *   *   *

"Current quotations for middling prompt shipment cotton classed
on government grade and staple standards and based on March futures
are:
                        *
           Inch and 1/8th - 225 to 275.
           Inch and 3/16ths - 375 to 450.
           Inch and 1/4th - 850 to 950."

Cotton News Letter of Feb. 3/'31 (p. 2)

QUOTATIONS ON PIMA AND EGYPTIAN COTTONS AT
NEW ENGLAND MILL POINTS RECEIVED BY
BUREAU OF AGRICULTURAL ECONOMICS

(Quotations on Sakel and Uppers are for medium grade only
and are duty paid)

Pima	January 30
No. 2	21.50 ¢
" 3	20.50
" 4	19.50

Sakel

Fully Good Fair . . . . 25.50 ¢

Uppers

Fully Good Fair . . . . 21.50 ¢

MIDDLING QUOTATION AT NEW ORLEANS

The closing quotation for Middling Spot cotton on the New Orleans market for January 30, as received by the Bureau of Agricultural Economics, was 10.16

LIVERPOOL PRICES OF EGYPTIAN AND UPLAND
COTTONS ON JANUARY 30.
(from Commercial and Financial Chronicle of January 31)

	1931 (pence) 1/	1930 (pence)	1929 (pence)
Good Sakel	9.55	15.10	19.70
Middling Uplands	5.63	8.85	10.35

1/ These prices correspond to prices at Liverpool on January 30 of 19.3 cents for Good Sakel and 11.3 cents for Middling Uplands, the pound sterling having been quoted at New York for cable transfer at $4.856 on January 30.

Cotton News Letter of Feb. 3/'31 (p. 3)

STOCKS AT ALEXANDRIA, EGYPT
(from Commercial and Financial Chronicle of January 31)

The stocks on January 30 of this year and of the two preceding years were as follows (Egyptian bales, average weight 750 pounds):

1931	1930	1929
713,000 bales	454,000 bales	461,000 bales

THE COTTON MARKET IN EGYPT.

"Cotton" of Manchester, issue of January 17, 1931, contains the following:

M. S. Casulli & Co., Alexandria, January 7th:-
*   *   *
"*** Maarad. - The decline of the Sakel contracts which has also affected those of Maarad attracts the attention of consumers, and the premiums rally vividly for all grades. *** "

Daniel, Pasquinelli & Co., Alexandria, January 8th -:
"Trading in this department is tending to expand, and both Maarad [Egyptian Pima] and Sakel are responsible for the improvement. The former is rapidly gaining favour with users, and the substantially larger supply anticipated for next season will find the market quite prepared to deal with it.
*   *

THE CROP IN EGYPT.

"Cotton" of Manchester, issue of January 17, 1931, contains the following:

Alexandria Commercial Co., Alexandria, January 8th:-
"Preparation of the land for the new crop has just commenced in a few districts; compared to last year, there is an appreciable delay in these operations. The projected law for the restriction of the acreage of Sakel has not yet been promulgated, and this is naturally unsettling to the growers in those districts affected by the proposed law."

Societe Cotonniere d'Egypte, S.A.E., Successeurs de la Maison G. D. Sarris, Alexandria, January 8th -:
"In Upper Egypt the preparation of the land for the new cotton has started, while in the Delta it is being done only in southern districts. The sale of seed for planting purposes is extremely slack, which is an indication of a drastic reduction of the acreage. We understand that the Government intends to provide small farmers with seed at favourable terms."

Washington, D. C.
February 3, 1931

EGYPTIAN COTTON NEWS LETTER
(Not for publication)

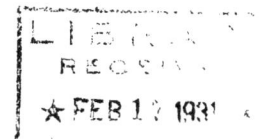

By Office of Egyptian Cotton Breeding, Bureau of Plant
Industry, U. S. Department of Agriculture

The information contained in this News Letter is drawn mainly from newspapers and trade journals, the published source of the information being given in every case. The object of the letter is to furnish information to officials and cooperators of the Department of Agriculture in regard to the condition of the market for long staple cotton. The Department assumes no responsibility for the accuracy and reliability of these quoted statements, and under no circumstances should they be republished as having been issued by the Department of Agriculture.

LONG STAPLE COTTON MARKET CONDITIONS

The New Bedford Standard of February 8 states as follows:

"Increased mill operations and considerably more active demand for staple cotton featured this and other New England cotton consuming centers during the past week, and trading in small lots was reported from many different quarters. With the exception of the large tire fabric mills there was not much buying in large quantity, but the large number of 100 and 200 bale sales made a respectable total at the close of the week.

"Some inquiry has been reported also for Pima cotton and sales of number ones and twos of good staple length were reported this week at 22 cents. Number twos have sold down as low as 18-1/2 cents within the past month, but the market is stiffer now, following stabilization attempts by several financial groups in the Southwest.

"Egyptians have been very quiet, with little or no change in nominal price quotations. This does not take into account a few odd bales of spots that have been cleaned up here and there at clean-up levels.

"Current quotations for middling prompt shipment staple Peelers classed on government grade and staple standards and based on March futures are:

        Inch and 1/8th - 225 to 275.
        Inch and 3/16ths - 375 to 450.
        Inch and 1/4th - 850 to 1,000."

Cotton News Letter of Feb. 10/'31 (p. 2)

QUOTATIONS ON PIMA AND EGYPTIAN COTTONS AT NEW ENGLAND MILL POINTS RECEIVED BY BUREAU OF AGRICULTURAL ECONOMICS

(Quotations on Sakel and Uppers are for medium grade only and are duty paid)

Pima	February 6
No. 2	22.75 ¢
" 3	21.75
" 4	20.75

Sakel

Fully Good Fair . . . . 25.75 ¢

Uppers

Fully Good Fair . . . . 21.75 ¢

MIDDLING QUOTATION AT NEW ORLEANS

The closing quotation for Middling Spot cotton on the New Orleans market for February 6, as received by the Bureau of Agricultural Economics, was 10.38

LIVERPOOL PRICES OF EGYPTIAN AND UPLAND COTTONS ON FEBRUARY 6.
(from Commercial and Financial Chronicle of February 7)

	1931 (pence)	1930 (pence)	1929 (pence)
	1/		
Good Sakel	9.70	14.60	17.95
Middling Uplands . . .	5.72	8.60	10.35

1/ These prices correspond to prices at Liverpool on February 6 of 19.6 cents for Good Sakel and 11.5 cents for Middling Uplands, the pound sterling having been quoted at New York for cable transfer at $4.860 on February 6.

Cotton News Letter of Feb. 10/'31 (p. 3)

STOCKS AT ALEXANDRIA, EGYPT
(from Commercial and Financial Chronicle of February 7)

The stocks on February 6 of this year and of the two preceding years were as follows (Egyptian bales, average weight 750 pounds):

1931	1930	1929
706,000 bales	460,000 bales	452,000 bales

THE COTTON MARKET IN EGYPT.

"Cotton" of Manchester, issue of January 24, 1931, contains the following dispatch from G. D. Economou & Co. of Alexandria, dated January 15:-

*   *   *

"There has been more activity in Sakellaridis also of late, and the same factor of shortage of arrivals is responsible for a rise in the premiums of the medium and higher grades. Maarad is much enquired for, and premiums therefor have stiffened to the extent of a dollar or more. It appears that there has been a good volume of business done in this growth, especially for India, and its limited production renders very difficult the question of the supply of this variety."

THE CROP IN EGYPT.

"Cotton" of Manchester, issue of January 24, contains the following dispatch from the Societe Cotonniere d'Egypte, S.A.E., Successeurs de la Maison Sarris, Alexandria, dated January 15:-

"The sale of sowing seed continues to be very slack, and the reduction of the Sakel acreage, in particular, seems to be a foregone conclusion. The money stringency up-country is, of course, the primary cause which, in addition, may render planters neglectful in their work. As the cultivation of Egyptian cotton needs great care and relatively high expenses, lack of funds may affect the crop adversely."

Washington, D. C.
February 10, 1931

EGYPTIAN COTTON NEWS LETTER
(Not for publication)

By Office of Egyptian Cotton Breeding, Bureau of Plant Industry, U. S. Department of Agriculture

The information contained in this News Letter is drawn mainly from newspapers and trade journals, the published source of the information being given in every case. The object of the letter is to furnish information to officials and cooperators of the Department of Agriculture in regard to the condition of the market for long staple cotton. The Department assumes no responsibility for the accuracy and reliability of these quoted statements, and under no circumstances should they be republished as having been issued by the Department of Agriculture.

LONG STAPLE COTTON MARKET CONDITIONS

The New Bedford Standard of February 15 states as follows:

"Buying interest continued active in most extra staple cotton consuming centers of New England during the past week and prices showed some improvement in certain quarters. It was still possible, however, to buy odd lots at the old minimum levels and in some types there was little stiffening in actual trading levels.

"Mills show some disposition to increase operating schedules but are seldom willing to buy in round lots for forward requirements. ***

"Considerable inquiry is reported for Pima cotton and the available supply seems to be tied up pretty well in the hands of one or two merchant firms. Prices continue easy, however, and small lots are moving at prices around 22 cents for twos and ones and 21 cents for twos and threes and 19 cents to 20 cents for threes and lower. Number ones of selected long staple are quoted around 23 cents to 25 cents but no sales at those levels are reported.

"Egyptians continue dull and inactive, with prices quoted nominally on the same basis, as previously.

"Current quotations on middling prompt shipment Peeler cotton classed on government grade and staple standards and based on March futures are:

    Inch and 1/8th - 225 to 275.
    Inch and 3/16ths - 400 to 450.
    Inch and 1/4th - 850 to 1,000."

Cotton News Letter of Feb. 17/'31 (p. 2)

QUOTATIONS ON PIMA AND EGYPTIAN COTTONS AT NEW ENGLAND MILL POINTS RECEIVED BY BUREAU OF AGRICULTURAL ECONOMICS

(Quotations on Sakel and Uppers are for medium grade only and are duty paid)

Pima	February 13
No. 2	23 ¢
" 3	22
" 4	21

Sakel

Fully Good Fair . . . . 26 ¢

Uppers

Fully Good Fair . . . . 23 ¢

MIDDLING QUOTATION AT NEW ORLEANS

The closing quotation for Middling Spot cotton on the New Orleans market for February 13, as received by the Bureau of Agricultural Economics, was 10.67

LIVERPOOL PRICES OF EGYPTIAN AND UPLAND COTTONS ON FEBRUARY 13.
(from Commercial and Financial Chronicle of February 14)

	1931 (pence)	1930 (pence)	1929 (pence)
	1/		
Good Sakel	10.05	14.55	19.65
Middling Uplands	5.85	8.69	10.43

1/ These prices correspond to prices at Liverpool on February 13 of 20.3 cents for Good Sakel and 11.8 cents for Middling Uplands, the pound sterling having been quoted at New York for cable transfer at $4.857 on February 13.

STOCKS AT ALEXANDRIA, EGYPT.
(from Commercial and Financial Chronicle of February 14)

The stocks on February 13 of this year and of the two preceding years were as follows (Egyptian bales, average weight 750 pounds):

1931	1930	1929
699,000 bales	467,000 bales	442,000 bales

MILL CONSUMPTION IN THE UNITED STATES OF PIMA AND IMPORTED EGYPTIAN COTTONS FOR JANUARY, 1931.

The Bureau of the Census reports mill consumption of American-Egyptian (Pima) cotton during the month of January as 1,238 bales of 500 pounds gross weight, compared with 898 bales in December and 779 bales in November. The mill consumption of imported Egyptian cotton is reported as having been 7,782 bales in January, compared with 10,104 bales in December and 9,076 bales in November.

REDUCTION OF SAKEL ACREAGE IN EGYPT.

The Agricultural Bulletin of Egypt (Bulletin de l'Union des Agriculteurs d'Egypte) No. 217, December, 1930, contains a statement which is here given in part (translation):

Sakellaridis is a type of cotton having special technical properties, hence its high price and restricted utilization.

The adaptation of the quantity produced to the average world consumption (approximately 150,000,000 pounds) therefore is well within the scope of the general cotton policy of the Government.

(Certain districts of three provinces in Lower Egypt are listed to which the Government proposes to confine future production of this variety).

The area of cotton in this region has never exceeded 630,000 acres and averages 580,000 acres, representing about 40 per cent of the total cultivated land in the region in question. This proportion is ample to assure production of 150,000,000 pounds of Sakellaridis.

In case of violation up to June 30, the authorities may order the plowing up of all Sakel in excess of the 40 per cent allowed. After this date, instead of destroying the plants, the illegal excess will be confiscated.

The reduction in the quantity of seed needed to plant the acreage as thus limited will make possible greater strictness as to the quality and purity of the planting seed. The character of the seeds suitable for planting will continue to be determined each year by the Ministry of Agriculture. No carryover of seeds for planting from one season to another will be permitted. Merchants may not sell the seeds to others than the licensed growers nor in quantity exceeding the legal limit.

These measures are to be in effect for three years, beginning with 1931.

from newspapers and trade journals, the published source of the information being given in every case. The object of the letter is to furnish information to officials and cooperators of the Department of Agriculture in regard to the condition of the market for long staple cotton. The Department assumes no responsibility for the accuracy and reliability of these quoted statements, and under no circumstances should they be republished as having been issued by the Department of Agriculture.

LONG STAPLE COTTON MARKET CONDITIONS

The New Bedford Standard of February 22 states as follows:

"Staple cotton prices began to harden all along the line during the past week, and there seemed to be less distressed cotton offering for sale. Although basis quotations on some types did not change materially, it was much more difficult to find offerings at the lower end of the price range than it was a week or two ago, and on some other types the prices were quotably higher by 25 to 50 points. ***

"Most mill men are now convinced that cotton has reached virtually its low point and that further substantial recessions from present levels can hardly be expected, but very few are willing to "buy now" against possible future needs. ***

"There has been very little demand for long staple Peeler cotton, but offerings have also been very few, and prices have continued unchanged.

"Good inquiry for Pima cotton, however, has been reported from many different quarters and prices have jumped up at least three cents this week even though the volume of sales has not been particularly heavy. Buying has taken place here, and also in Providence and some of the other New England markets. Pima No. 1s, which sold a week or two ago around 22-1/2 cents, have now been marked up to 25-1/2 cents and it is virtually impossible to buy any cheaper. Number twos are priced around 24 cents to 24-1/2 cents and can not be had any lower, while number threes are priced around 23 cents.

"Egyptians are also somewhat higher, and medium grade Sakellaridis is now quoted around 28 cents to 29 cents with only very occasional lots available below these levels. High grade Sakels are commanding 29 cents or even 30 cents if the staple length is unusually good. Uppers have been inactive for the week.

Cotton News Letter of Feb. 25/'31 (p. 2)

tement relative to long staple cotton market continued:

"Current quotations on middling prompt shipment Peeler cotton classed on government grade and staple standards and based on May futures are:

* *
Inch and 1/8th - 250 to 275.
Inch and 3/16ths - 425 to 475.
Inch and 1/4th - 900 to 1,000."

QUOTATIONS ON PIMA AND EGYPTIAN COTTONS AT
NEW ENGLAND MILL POINTS RECEIVED BY
BUREAU OF AGRICULTURAL ECONOMICS

(Quotations on Sakel and Uppers are for medium grade only and are duty paid)

Pima	February 20
No. 2	25 ¢
" 3	24
" 4	23

Sakel

Fully Good Fair . . . . 26.60 ¢

Uppers!

Fully Good Fair . . . . 23.00 ¢

MIDDLING QUOTATION AT NEW ORLEANS

The closing quotation for Middling Spot cotton on the New Orleans market for February 20, as received by the Bureau of Agricultural Economics, was 10.69

LIVERPOOL PRICES OF EGYPTIAN AND UPLAND
COTTONS ON FEBRUARY 20.
(from Commercial and Financial Chronicle of February 21)

	1931 (pence)	1930 (pence)	1929 (pence)
Good Sakel	10.40 1/	14.35	19.10
Middling Uplands . . .	6.04	8.47	10.49

1/ These prices correspond to prices at Liverpool on February 20 of 21.0 cents for Good Sakel and 12.2 cents for Middling Uplands, the pound sterling having been quoted at New York for cable transfer at $4.855 on February 20.

Cotton News Letter of Feb. 25/'31 (p. 3)

STOCKS AT ALEXANDRIA, EGYPT.
(from Commercial and Financial Chronicle of February 21)

The stocks on February 20 of this year and of the two preceding years were as follows (Egyptian bales, average weight 750 pounds):

1931	1930	1929
695,000 bales	473,000 bales	439,000 bales

EGYPTIAN COTTON IMPORTS

The Bureau of the Census reports as follows the imports from Egypt, in equivalent 500-pound bales, during the month of January and during the 6 months ending January 31, 1931, as well as the corresponding data for the preceding year:

January		:	6 months ending January 31	
1931	1930	:	1931	1930
2,541	23,128	:	3,582	98,778

THE CROP IN EGYPT

"Cotton" of Manchester, issue of February 7, 1931, contains the following dispatch from the Societe Cotoniere d'Egypte, S.A.E., Successeurs de la Maison G. D. Sarris, of Alexandria, dated January 29th:-

*   *   *

"As regards the next crop, land preparations are being carried out on most economic lines, and the sale of seed for planting is still slow on long credit terms. The reduction of acreage for the Sakel growth in any case seems inevitable, but it is yet too early to estimate to what extent, and it transpires that spinners' delegates who are in Alexandria just now are not adverse to a measure to that effect from the Government should the latter undertake to gradually dispose of its holdings after the present season is out."

Washington, D. C.
February 25, 1931

tton news letter
es Bureau of Plant Industry;United States. Bureau of Pl
999_131
ment of Agriculture, National Agricultural Library
ptiancottonn1931unit_0
4

CPSIA information can be obtained
at www.ICGtesting.com
Printed in the USA
LVHW081048141118
596964LV00009B/355/P